BETWEEN LOST & FOUND

"Germaine Smith's book is refreshingly honest and filled with real-world wisdom. It will be of great benefit to those recovering from abuse but also for each and every person who is on an honest walk toward wholeness. The stories and tools she shares equip us to face the pain in our lives with hope and integrity."

—Christopher Ranweiler,
Director of Campus Ministry, Hill-Murray School

"When you are wounded by abuse and imprisoned by grief, guilt, and hatred, how can healing begin? This is a practical and poetic guide for healing and wholeness written from experience and from the heart. Each chapter's reflections remind us that we are not alone in our struggle to reclaim our truth, our voice, and our dignity. The exercises provide helpful and doable steps forward in the journey toward wholeness. I recommend this guide as a hopeful starting place for anyone in need of healing."

—Melissa Johnson, parent and friend of loved ones struggling with addiction and depression

"I was profoundly moved and inspired by Germaine Smith's journey of recovery in *Between Lost & Found*. Her honesty and courage in facing her past and her emphasis on the importance of healing speak to all of us on our own journeys."

—Paul Deziel, Religious Educator and Youth Minister, Guardian Angels Catholic Church

BETWEEN LOST & FOUND

a guide to finding
Wholeness
after Abuse

Germaine Smith

The Center
For Healing
Press

© 2014 by Germaine Smith. All rights reserved.

Cover photo: © icando, www.fotosearch.com
Cover and page design: Ann Delgehausen, Trio Bookworks

ISBN: 978-0-9960421-0-9 (print)

All rights reserved. No portion of this publication may be reproduced or transmitted in any form or by any means, electronic or mechanical, including photocopying, recording, or capturing on any information storage and retrieval system, without permission in writing from the publisher, except by a reviewer who may quote brief passages in a critical article or review to be printed in a magazine or newspaper, or electronically transmitted on radio, television, or the Internet.

For reprint permission, email germ@thecenterforhealing.us.

The Center For Healing Press is the imprint of The Center For Healing, a spirituality school for those seeking wholeness. If you are looking for someone to accompany you on your journey to wholeness, Germaine Smith serves as a spiritual guide and teacher. She can help you discover the answers you need for your own journey to wholeness. Contact her at germ@thecenterforhealing.us.

Life is a paradox.

I have raised myself
and
I have been raised by countless hands that got me to this time and space.

I have been formed by those who have loved me
and
those who have refused to love me.

I do everything by myself
and
I do nothing alone.

I dedicate this
to all who are discovering the need to heal their little kids
and
to the two women who helped me discover and heal mine:

Denise Hanna Bisanz
and
Mary Anna Palmer

In Gratitude

Thanks to Mary McPherson, Jonathan Sweet, Beth Wallace,
and all at Trio Bookworks for their expertise in publishing this book.

Contents

Prologue	xi

1
LOST — 1

Lost	3
The Little Children	5
Finding Help	8
Hero	11
You First	13
You Are Ready	15
Start Where You Are ⚡	17

2
The WOUNDING — 19

The Wounding	21
Your Particular Hell	23
Victimization	25
Bravery	27
Unnatural Escape Routes	29
Taking Inventory ⚡	31

3
SUCKING SILT

33	
35	Sucking Silt
38	Beyond Victimization
41	The Abusers
44	If You Have Abused Someone
46	Changing the Channel
48	At the Edge
50	Scars
52	Self-Work
54	Releasing Captives
57	Playing in Hell ♒

4
CLIMBING
the MOUNTAIN

59	
61	Climbing the Mountain
65	Paradox of Life
67	Never-Ending Memories
69	Shake the Dust from Your Feet
72	Taking a Break
74	♒ Wants and Needs

5
RIDING the WAVES of HEALING 75

Riding the Waves of Healing	77
Healing Comes in Many Colors	79
Healing the Body	81
Twenty-Three Ways to Nurture the Body	84
Healing the Heart	86
Facing Fear	89
Welcoming Serenity	91
Embracing Depression	93
The Joy of Joy	95
Forgiving Guilt	97
Laughter	99
Expressing Anger	100
Healthy Ways to Be Angry	102
The Gift of Acceptance	104
Experiencing Grief Uncovered	106
Wide Openness	109
Admitting Hatred and Knowing Compassion	111
Releasing Shame, Encountering Dignity	113
The Serial Killer Called Resentment	114
Healing the Mind	116
The Reality of Brainwashing	118
A Plentitude of Affirmations	120
When All Else Fails	122
Healing the Soul	124
The Dina Story	127

129	The "No Visions, No Voices" Story
131	Praying
133	Working Your Way to Wholeness ⌇

6
The ART *of* INTEGRATION

135	
137	The Meaning of Integration
139	✣✣✣
140	Where Memories Go
142	Friends and Enemies
143	When I Was Young
145	Different Worlds
149	Speaking Wholeness
150	⌇ Living Consciously

7
The PROMISED LAND

151	
152	The Promised Land
154	The Promised Land's Reflection of Truth
156	Rural Minnesota
158	My Creed
159	Found
161	Healing the World ⌇

Prologue

I was abused.
   And lost.
   And didn't know it
     because I sought escape
     at the bottom of a bottle of brandy.

What I did know was something was drastically wrong
   within me.
   I felt worthless, incomplete.
I never felt whole.
Instead, the opposite was true:
   I felt hatred for who I was.

When I saw my first therapist in 1987
I told her I wasn't afraid of the dark—
I was afraid of the light.

It felt like a door had opened just a crack
and the light breaking in was too bright
   too powerful
   too illuminating
   far too exposing.

I was both fearful of the light and drawn to it
   because I instinctively knew that
   out of darkness
   all things are born
     especially truth.

As I worked my way through therapy
I came to see my healing as a cleaning out of my karmic house.
I had this old house within me
   with many rooms filled with memories of horror and pain
     each needing to be brought out
     into the light.

As I brought my childhood past out of the house,
I set each memory and all its baggage in the courtyard
   to be evaluated.
   What did I want or need to reclaim?
   What did I want or need to release?

The journey for me became an owning:
   owning myself through owning my past.

It was a long, arduous, and often desperate journey
   fraught with such horrific revelations
     that I longed to abandon the house—
     never to breach its doorway again.

But slowly the light overcame my memories
   and I began to experience something other than hatred:
     a glimpse of wholeness.

I began to write this chronology of my healing
    as a way to give my "kids" a voice.
I was taught in therapy that each person has within them
    children from all the ages of their life.
We all have within us a two-year-old seeking identity
    as well as a sixteen-year-old demanding independence
    in addition to all the other ages we have experienced.

Most well-adjusted adults are not conscious of these little kids
    except in recalling a happy or sad event from childhood.
    A well-adjusted adult probably has well-adjusted little kids.

For those who have been abused, our adulthood is a struggle
    because of the suffering of the children within us.
As wounded adults, we seek recovery
    from all that pain from our past.

Healing is the art of acknowledging our wounded children,
    listening to their stories,
    and then helping them to recover their wholeness
    so we can live as whole adults.

This is a story of healing
    not a tale of abuse.
I do not wish to dwell on or recount
    the details of my abuse for this book.
        That's a private—not a public—conversation.

I don't wish to be the poster child for abuse.
I wish to be the beacon for recovery and wholeness.

And what I offer through this book
   is a view of the journey.

This is a story of my journey.
   I offer it as a guide.
But each person must take their own journey.
If this guide aids you in yours, wonderful.
If you require something different, wonderful.
   The key is to listen to what you need to heal.

My journey was a healing in four aspects of my life:
   physical, emotional, mental, and spiritual.

On a physical level, my healing required
   that I admit my many addictions
   and begin a program of recovery.
Respecting my body was essential
   because it had been so disrespected
   throughout my childhood.

On an emotional level, psychotherapy helped me uncover
   the memories of abuse
   and deal with all the often overwhelming and
   contradictory emotions.
From childhood through early adulthood, I was numb.
Learning to feel and then deal with all the emotions
   of the buried memories was vital.

On a mental level, I was challenged to change my thinking:
    eliminate thoughts of worthlessness and unimportance
    and learn how to honor and love myself.
Recognizing and replacing old, negative programming
    with the truth about the value of my identity
    and individuality
    was imperative.

On a spiritual level, my healing was most significant.
    My first spiritual obstacle was:
        Who am I as a spiritual person?

I came to understand that I am both body and soul—
    that the soul is my connection to God
    the part of me that is God.
I am not the totality of this Higher Power.
    I have many limitations as a human person
    but God and I are one—
        we share the same energy of the soul.

Spirituality is the art of embracing the connection
    that I have with God.
    This is a birthright—
    to be in relationship with a Power greater than myself.

My second spiritual obstacle was:
    What kind of God did I believe in?

I was taught to obey a demanding God,
   who punishes through abuse,
   whose identity mirrored that of the father and mother
   I grew up with.
   This vision of God was not healthy for me.

I released the image of God as Father
   and myself as wayward child,
   of God as Judge and myself as woeful sinner.
I came to believe in and then claim a Power greater than myself
   a God that is Wholeness.
My job as a human person is to realize my wholeness
   as part of the greater Wholeness.

Because language is limiting
   I use a variety of names for this Higher Power:
     God, the Divine, Energy,
     Pure Consciousness, Truth, the Universe,
     Wisdom.
The names we choose are important; language is powerful.
   Using a variety of words helps me
   to remember that God is indefinable.
This book reflects both my philosophy and my theology
   about the spiritual life.
Each chapter of this work speaks the truth
   of my journey through abuse.
At the end of every chapter are exercises:
   suggestions of ways to heal the body, mind, heart, and soul.

I have intentionally varied the order of these four
    because they are all equally important.
    There is no hierarchy of healing in the journey.

For example, when I began the journey of my healing
    recovery from drug addiction had to be my first step.
    Healing my body came first.
But in the next stage of healing from my abuse,
    dealing with my emotional pain took priority.
In other words, in each phase
    I listened for what aspect of healing—
    physical, mental, emotional, or spiritual,—
        needed to be the priority.
And the priority changed as I healed.
Throughout the journey,
    listening is key.

Unfortunately, abuse is common in our world.
It comes in many forms—
    neglect, abandonment,
    using love as a tool for control or manipulation,
    hate-filled words,
    slaps, punches, beatings,
    unwanted sexual touching, rape.

No matter what age we are when the abuse occurs
    there is wounding.
The pain from that experience will not go away
    no matter how much we deny it or ignore it
    or medicate ourselves.

The only way is through it.

Recovery from abuse is not only possible
    but a journey worth the effort.
It is the path to freedom
    an adventure in finding yourself
    a journey to wholeness.

May all who are scared of the light
    find the courage to open the door to their past
    and
    give birth to their truth.

1

LOST

Lost

Everyone in the world is lost.
Most do not even know it.
Many know it and deny it.
Some seek to understand but can't figure it out.
Few get found.

Some hide behind jobs, or titles, or other people,
    thinking position or obscurity
    will protect them from the truth.
Some hide their pasts in locked vaults
    hoping the truth inside is impenetrable.
Eventually, both solutions are temporary, unsatisfying,
    and unhealthy.

Being lost is part of living.
Things happen, and we lose our way.
Being found is also part of this life.
It is the path of courage and strength and endurance.

Being found is not about someone else finding you.
It is not about having a savior, in any form, rescue you.

We all get lost
    but the difficult part is that no person,
    no material item can save us.
Either we are our own hero, or we stay lost.

This book is for those lost because of abuse.
Whether physical or sexual, mental or emotional,
    abuse wreaks havoc with our ability to be healthy and whole.
Most of us are lost and yearn to be found.

Being found is a state of being, of knowing who you are.
It is the ultimate goal that every human being shares:
    to know who we are at our core.

Are you one who knows they are lost
    and are willing to do what needs to be done to be found?

Welcome home.

The Little Children

No matter what your chronological age
   you have little children inside you
   from your past—
   little kids who are you.

They are your past and can heal your present
   and will build your future.
They just need your attention.

They have been deeply wounded but have survived.
Be gentle with them.
Love them tenderly.
Protect them fiercely.
   They need your help to heal.

Sometimes they will refuse to speak
   and you will experience the dead silence of pain.
Sometimes they will all speak at the same time
   and you will have fifteen voices clamoring at once.
Give each their time. That is all they need.

Everyone has little children, even the most well-adjusted.
Those of us abused have little kids who
    act out, withdraw, throw temper tantrums,
    get weepy, peace-make,
    people-please, laugh inappropriately, pout,
    get belligerent, get clingy,
    stand too close, never hug, never laugh, are lost.

Be gentle with them.
They will heal.
Slowly,
with love.

They have great memories, and horrific memories to share.
    You need to let them.

They have been shut down and shut out for a long time.
Now that they have found you, they will not let go.

Please don't try to shut off their voices.
    That is not the path to healing or health.
    It will just deepen the pain and lengthen the process.

When you have given your inner children the voice needed,
    you will hear their panicked cries less and less.

At some point, you may not hear from them for a long time.
    Integration has begun.
    This is how you know they are healing.

Until then, give them time and attention.

As you give them their voice, they will find a place of rest
    in you.

Finding Help

You will do this work by yourself, and you cannot do it alone.
You will need help, and that help will present itself
 when you are ready.

Recognizing the right help is challenging and essential.
Trust yourself and your needs.

Know that when you are ready, the healer will be ready.

This will probably be a long-term, intimate relationship.
Consider what you want; demand what you need.

Probably this help will include a mental health professional.
There are the obvious inquiries:
 Male or female?
 Racial background?
 Sexual orientation or acceptance of GLBT people?
 Do spirituality or religious connections matter?
 Marriage and family therapist or psychologist or psychiatrist?
 Working independently or with an organization?
 Does age matter?
 Cost?

In the end, the person you choose will be walking beside you
on your journey.
They are not the expert on your journey—you are.

Their expertise lies in their ability to carry out two tasks.

1) Build and hold the two-way street of trust.
As a survivor, this is probably not your strong suit.
Work on it.
The greater the trust, the deeper the healing.
In order to do that, your therapist also needs to share.
This is a relationship, not a business transaction.
Ask questions.
The best therapists are honest enough
to share their humanity
without losing sight of their role.
They are secure enough in both
their professional competence
and their personal identity
to build a trusting relationship with you.
Weave that bond of trust between you.
You need that trust when the memories are overwhelming.

Without trust, the walls of protective silence stay in place.
Trust is the gateway to giving your kids and the memories
a voice.

2) Hold the container.
This is the most important task of any therapist or healer.
And it is probably the least identified or taught.

Your job is to bring memories and emotions to the light,
    so they can be named and owned, then claimed or released.
Your therapist's job is to create a space
    where all that energy can be safely examined.
Holding that container requires great skill and compassion.
    She or he cannot do any of the work that is yours.
When the therapist skillfully holds the container
    of powerful and often conflicting emotions,
    you can securely work with the past
    and safely return to the present.

Trust your instincts in this job of finding help.
Do not be afraid to release and move on
    if one therapist doesn't work out.
    Just make sure you're not running away,
    seeking an escape from the work.

Do not be discouraged if you get fired by a therapist.
    Sometimes they have not done enough
        of their own work to know how to help.
    Pick yourself up and know that someone else
        is going to be available.

When you find one that works, be grateful.
Say "thank you" often.
Therapy is a healing art,
    an honorable and dignity-restoring vocation.
You are both embarking on an incredible journey through hell
and, God willing, she or he will hold your hand all the way
    through to the other side.

Hero

I am not your hero
    nor do I wish to be.

Being someone else's hero only begets egotism and false pride
    and I cannot afford those.
They are too great a temptation
    to wallow in self-centered falsehood
    that I am someone else's savior, rescuer, hero.

Hero worship is attractive
    because it detracts from the work at hand,
    which always is to focus on self.
It is inauthentic
    because it promotes a belief
    that the hero is perfect, flawless, invincible.

I am not your hero
    just a woman who has survived hell
    and found the promised land of knowing who I am.

Often our little kids want to be rescued.
    We want the superhero to swoop in and save us.

That is the fairy tale.
In real life, you cannot look to others to be your hero
   nor can you rescue someone else.

So do not search for heroes outside yourself.
Look in the mirror and see yourself
   as the only one who can truly rescue your kids.

You are lost until
   you become your own hero.

You First

There will come a time when
   family, career, friends, drugs, sex, home,
   popularity, food, clothes,
   reputation, security, relationships, status,
   acceptance, masks, falsehoods
     are not enough.
Pray you have reached that time.

When you begin to know on a gut level that you come first
   then finally you are ready.

In the beginning, we all try to put other people or things first.
We have been taught it is the "right" thing,
   the charitable thing to do.
But it is neither of those things.

No one can authentically, with integrity, put others first
   until that person knows who she or he actually is.
That is the task of recovery.
Trying to put others first until you know who you are
   will not be enough.
     And it never will be.

It's like the safety message on an airplane:
    You must put on your own oxygen mask
    before trying to assist others.

In time, when you are healed,
    balance will return and be genuine.
In time, you will be both willing and able to put others first
    and help them on their journey.

For now, recovery is your main—perhaps your solo—task.

You need to find you,
    to heal the broken you.

And you are worth the effort.

You Are Ready

If memories are starting to poke
through your vast system of denial
you are ready.

They may be vague, blurry, ambiguous feelings
that something is not "right."
The truth is, if the memories are starting,
you are ready.

You cannot prepare for this journey.

Its timing is often when the soul determines the body is ready.
And the soul will push and pull
and drag and jerk with all its resources
to break through the denial of your abuse.
The soul knows this is the path to truth.

Fighting it will not help.

With each memory faced and embraced
you make more room for your soul
and more space for your truth.

It is time to reclaim yourself.
It is time to be whole again.

You are ready.

Start Where You Are

The exercises are suggestions about ways to help
bring healing and wholeness
to all aspects of your being.
Use what you like; leave the rest.
There is no "right" or "wrong" way to heal.
Just start where you are.

Physical
If you are abusing any chemicals, reach out to AA, NA, or another
 recovery program.
If you are being abused, reach out for help now.
Identify some healthy ways to give your body security and comfort:
 name some foods, some activities, some ways to rest, etc.

Emotional
Make a list of the places in your life where you feel lost.
Be gentle and aware, not critical or judgmental.
Remember some times in your life when you felt "found."
Savor those memories.
Consider finding a therapist.
Are there any nonnegotiable elements for your therapist?
Promise yourself you can and will find someone to help.

Mental
Make a list of people who could be of support to you.
Make a timeline of your childhood at ages five, eight, twelve,
 and sixteen.
  What games or toys or activities did you like?
  How did you spend an average Saturday afternoon?
Put together a playlist of songs that inspire you on this journey.

Spiritual
Expand your conscious contact with the Divine.
What are your doubts and truths about the Divine?
Begin a daily mantra or affirmation practice, such as
 "I am seeking wholeness in all areas of my life."

2

The WOUNDING

The Wounding

You have been wounded.
The memories are starting to poke through
    like stretching a seam until it rips from the fabric.

You feel—maybe for the first time.
It does not matter your age.
    You are ready.

Trust the memories.
    (Repeat this line as often as necessary.)

Whatever you feel or sense, let it speak to you.

You are not crazy.
You are not making it up.

This is real.

The memories will not go away.
They are you.
They are your truth.

Yes, your life is going to fall completely apart.
You are strong enough to do this work.
Yes, you are entering a realm of hell
    filled with suffering and pain.
You are brave enough to do this work.

You have survived the abuse.
Yes, you will survive the recovery.

And yes, you will get to the other side.

Your Particular Hell

Single perpetrator or multiple offenders
abuser known to you as a "friend" or relative
    or personally unknown to you
solitary incident or continuous abuse over many years
outwardly without injury or broken flesh and bone
done under the guise of "love" or in a fit of rage
in privacy or in front of others.

On the one hand, the circumstances of your abuse
    do not really matter.
Your particular hell is just that—your particular hell.
You will have to identify your particular hell's regions
    and participants and motives
    in order to deal with them.
And whatever the answers, the healing journey will follow
    a similar path.

On the other hand, your particular hell is *your* particular hell.
It is unique to you and
    you will have to discover your individual method
    of traveling this road.

This road to your particular hell.

I give you the sagest advice I ever heard in therapy
    regarding this hellish abyss you are about to transverse:

"Take as much time as you need and do it as fast as you can."*

---

* Mary Anna Palmer, psychotherapy sessions, 1996–1997.

Victimization

You were hurt.
   Someone caused you pain
      by invading your body, mind, soul.
         You can heal it.

You were abused.
   Someone violated
      your trust
      your sense of well-being.
         You can restore it.

You were robbed.
   Someone stole
      childhood essentials
      of innocence
      of joy
      of playfulness
      of wonder.
         You can return them.

You were murdered.
   Someone killed your spirit
      your dreams
      your hopes.
         You can resurrect them.

You were a victim.
You are a fighter.
   Someone stole your life as it should have been.
      TAKE IT BACK.

Bravery

Bravery is the ability to go toward what you fear.
As a child, you perhaps did not have the opportunity
   to be publicly brave.
     You could not confront your abusers.
     You could not stop them.
You were a child.
Standing up to the forces of your abuse meant more abuse
   or even death.

You were brave because you endured the abuse
   without letting it win.
You were brave
   when you fought for sheer survival in the hope
   that someday you could heal.

You did what you had to do in order to survive.
   At times you acquiesced
   or cooperated,
     perhaps even participated with your abuser.
Whatever you did, you did it to survive.

The little kids in you were brave.
Enduring hell is a feat of great courage.

As an adult, your bravery is confirmed by your choice
    to walk this path.
Facing the past—the past in its totality—takes bravery.
Not all wish to shine the light of truth
    into all the corners of hell.

But you have made the decision and are facing yourself.

And you will do what needs to be done
    to shine the light of truth
    not just on the actions of others
    but to confront the corners of your own fear.

No other person may know or comprehend the depth
    of your bravery.
That doesn't matter.
You know the courage this path takes.

And it will carry you to the other side—to wholeness.

Unnatural Escape Routes

There are few good options for escaping this hell
   when we are young.
Children have no money, no power, no independence.
If we run
   living on the streets or cycling through foster care is likely.
Most of us stay at our homes of origin for lack of better options.
But we often are desperately in need of some form of escape.

Some of us choose to become just like the abuser
   stealing power from anyone we can
      so we feel what we think is proper for adults: domination.
Some of us choose to hide within ourselves,
   lost souls who give away power and voice
      to become empty shells.
Many of us find an addiction to soothe our unconscious pain.
   Almost anything works:
      sex, gambling, shopping, exercise, fantasy, video games,
      and all manner of new technologies.
But the most popular escape
   for the last one hundred plus years
   is drug use.

We crave the escape
>   that alcohol and legal and illegal drugs provide.
>   They let us hide behind masks of unconsciousness
>   and allow us to be numb.

As children, unnatural escape routes were probably
>   our only respite.
But in adulthood it is time to grow up and be real,
>   and being real is what we fear the most.

Despite all the help available, recovery is still difficult
>   and demanding.
But you cannot recover from your abuse
>   until you recover from whatever unhealthy behaviors
>   and addictions you own.
Those behaviors may have served you in the past,
>   but their usefulness has concluded.

All unhealthy routes have the same destination:
>   unconsciousness and unfeeling.
That's what makes them unhealthy and unnatural.

Taking Inventory

As you review the following, do not judge yourself at all.
Just take an inventory.
Pledge to pay attention.
Become more aware of your present state of being.

Physical
Take inventory of your physical health.
How does your wounding manifest itself in your body?
If it feels safe for you, keep a log for five days of everything you eat or drink.
What does it tell you about your state of physical health?
What types of exercise do you enjoy?

Mental
Take inventory of your mental health.
How does your wounding manifest itself in your mind?
Keep a log for five days of anything you take or do to be "numb."
What does it tell you about your state of mental health?
How often each day are you in the present moment?

Spiritual
Take inventory of your spiritual health.
How does your wounding manifest itself in your soul?
What are your three most important beliefs about the Divine?
Keep a log for five days of how you "feed" your soul.
What does it tell you about your state of spiritual health?

Emotional
Take inventory of your emotional health.
How does your wounding manifest itself in your heart and in your relationships?
Keep a log for five days of how you express your emotions.
What does it tell you about your state of emotional health?
How would you rank your stress level today?

3

SUCKING SILT

Sucking Silt

The memories come.
You have been hit with 1,000 volts of hypersensitivity
and
you have been dropped in a zero-visibility fog
at the same time.

You feel everything, and you don't have a clue where you are.

Time melts together.
The memories of the past
and the reality of the present
and the anticipation of the future
all blur.

You have been swamped by a tidal wave of emotion
and it sinks you to the nethermost region of the river floor.

It is not just that you are drowning in all this emotion;
in trying to breathe,
you are sucking silt off the murky, muddy bottom.

Ugly memories that leave permanent scars announce
    themselves as your truth
but right now you are a long way from producing scar tissue.

Right now, with each announcement, you are struggling:
    what you thought you had is gone
    to be replaced by what you do not know.

Equilibrium is lost, and you wrestle in the current for stability
    that does not come.
Right now your wound is gaping and getting larger
and you can't get off the bottom.

All you can do is inhale the silt of your memories
    and hope they don't choke you.

Sometimes the memories will
    choke off your hope, your desire to survive.
Sometimes you just swallow the vile ugliness of your memories
    like a bad-tasting medicine.

Sucking silt is the worst stage
It's dark and foul, and you're drowning
and from this position you cannot see the end.

No end to the memories.
    You'll wonder how they could possibly be true.
    Maybe you dreamed them?
    Maybe you just made it all up?

No end to the horror.
    Maybe you'll try to convince yourself
        that you are the one who is sick, not your abusers.
    Maybe try to believe the abuse wasn't that bad,
        try to paint it over with a thick coat of denial.

No end to the emotions.
    Fear, panic, anxiety get replaced with
    shame, guilt, embarrassment get replaced with
    hatred, loathing, depression get replaced with
    fear, panic, anxiety get replaced with . . .

So here are the facts about sucking silt:
Yes, it will end.
Yes, the only way is through,
    the only way to wholeness is to recover
    and own the memories of your past.
    Do not try to circumvent or negate it.
Yes, it really did happen.
    Do not try to deny or minimize it.

Yes, it is horrible and ugly.
But it is not the totality of you.
    Abuse is part of you. Part of your experience.
Yes, you will get through this and heal.

Yes, it will end.

Beyond Victimization

Yes, you are a victim.
Don't wear it like a neon billboard
   announcing to the world your history
   as if the world owes you something.

The only ones who get to claim their victimhood are children.
Children are victims without disclaimer.
They have no power.
They must accept what is given
   and what is taken without any recourse.
They have no authority to end the abuse.

No way out.
Children have only two options:
   1) rely on the justice of others
   or
   2) survive until adulthood, when they can empower
      themselves to heal.

Once you reach chronological adulthood, you are responsible:
   responsible for healing
   responsible for your adulthood in behavior as well as age.

It is tempting to play the victim
    to think you are entitled to be taken care of by everyone else.
You are not.
You are not entitled to that type of arrogance.
Wean yourself off the pacifier of victimhood:
    Resist saying, "I can't."
    Stop expecting others to do your work.
    Refuse to be enabled.

Yes, justice was absent for you.
But don't wear your victimhood like a welcome mat,
    inviting anyone who passes to wipe their feet
    and leave you covered in mud.

Learn to stand,
    to set healthy boundaries,
        to hold them.

Your heart has no protection,
    so others feel they can abuse you any time.

Put up a stop sign.
    Ticket those who drive right through.

If they refuse to respect your limits
    take away their license to drive down your street.
    End the relationship you have
    with those who don't respect you.

Yes, a horrible thing happened to you.
Don't wear it like a coat of armor
    knocking down other living things you come in contact with
        because you are mad, sad, hurt, or confused.

Your abuse stopped your growth.
That's an explanation,
    not an excuse for your own bad behavior.

It is tempting to play the victim,
    to think you are entitled to be mean
    because you were abused.
You are not.
You are not entitled to act like a jackass to those around you.

Perhaps your heart is closed, encased.
Now is the time to un-build
    your self-defense wall of protection.
Start slowly, one brick at a time.
    You can even keep the bricks close by
        until you realize you don't need them all.

Yes, you are a victim.
But that word does not define you.

So where are you allowing yourself to be a victim?
    Don't abuse yourself further with judgment;
    awareness is the first step.

Being a victim is where you start—but not where you end.

The Abusers

The person or persons who hurt you are wounded.

This is not an excuse—it is a fact.
It does not change their responsibility for the pain they inflicted
   and the innocence they stole from you.
You can hate them, even wish them dead.
   It's okay to think that,
      especially in the beginning.

You can put their pictures on a dart board,
   punch them out on your punching bag,
   scream at them in the basement with the windows closed,
   write them letters you don't send,
   demanding your dignity back,
   have fantasy funerals and bury them.

Whatever you feel is okay—
acting on those feelings is not.

Own what you feel about them.
   It might be anger, fear, hatred.
   Or it might be pity, sadness, or even love.

Feelings are not your totality.
>   They are part of you but do not have to control you.
>   They just ask to be recognized and owned as part of you.
>   The process of doing that will give these feelings rest.

It will take time. This is not a quick-fix problem.
>   But your feelings will heal
>   if you give them air and attention.

Own what you feel. Name it. Claim it. Feel it.
These feelings do not make you the same as the abuser.
>   They are just feelings.

In reality, your abuser felt powerless,
>   angry, lost, lonely, afraid . . .
>   and turned those feelings on you.

They were probably abused
>   and repeated a learned behavior
>>   because they didn't know any different way to act.

Again, this is not an excuse—just a fact.
It does not change their responsibility for the pain they inflicted
>   and the innocence they stole from you.

They were wounded, and they wounded you.
>   They continued the cycle of pain.

What they did was wrong on all levels.
>   It is a criminal act.

Consider if you want to press charges.
Consider if you want to confront them.
There is not "right" or "wrong"—
   just what is healthy for you.
Know that the best revenge is a fabulous recovery.

You are not the abuser.
The way to break the cycle is to knowv that you are wounded
   and healing those wounds.

Healing will happen—it's a guarantee—
   if you face your past
   and let Light touch these wounds you have spent a lifetime
   trying to bury.

Secrets kill.
Silence feeds the cycle of abuse.
Speaking, naming the truth heals.

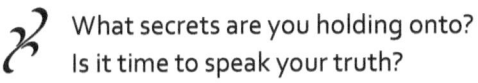
What secrets are you holding onto?
Is it time to speak your truth?

If You Have Abused Someone

If you have abused another human being or an animal,
    recognize it as part of the destructive pattern
    in the cycle of abuse.

That action is always unhealthy, damaging, criminal.
It is also familiar.

We repeat patterns we know
    and most of us don't know any other patterns except abuse.
It doesn't make us evil, but it does make us abusers
    and that is one thing we can change.

Abuse is a learned behavior. We can un-learn it.
We can learn better patterns of behavior. We can change.

Are you currently abusing someone?

If you are:
    Make a contract with yourself to stop immediately.
    Find a therapist. Immediately.
    Call 911.

You are wounded—
   inflicting wounds on another will not heal yours.
This is the time to protect another,
   to be an adult.

You are not evil, but this behavior must never happen again.

There is a way out. Ask for help.
Immediately.

Changing
the Channel

You have been programmed
    with many false and often crippling messages.
It is now time to name them so you can change them.

Changing the programming is possible
    only if you acknowledge what is playing
    on the present channel.

One strong message you may have received unequivocally was
    "Don't tell anyone."
The abuser required a code of silence
    in order to continue abusing.
    This programming is serving only the abuser;
    silence never heals the one abused.

"No one will believe you" is a line
    that may have kept you feeling powerless.
    You were a child;
    of course you thought no one would believe your words
    over an adult's denial.

You may feel the weight of having to protect "the family."
The abusers used your loyalty and love of family
   to convince you
      that keeping the secrets was more important
      than your well-being.

Know that by the act of sharing your abuse
   and breaking the code of secrets,
   you are healing.
Know that speaking out is the path to wholeness.

Know that you will be believed—
   perhaps not by everyone
      because some people are not willing or able
      to face the truth.
   You will be believed by those who love you
      and, most importantly,
      you can believe yourself.

Know you are not responsible for protecting the adults
   who abused you.
   You are responsible for healing yourself.

Know that challenging and changing these messages
   is the path to wholeness.

At
the Edge

You will stand at the edge of the great abyss and wish to die.
Death seems like such an accommodating answer—
   no more memories
   therefore no more pain.
The wound is excruciating; death seems like the only way out.

Just know: thinking of suicide is not a natural state of mind;
   nor is suicide a natural activity for the body.
And it is definitely not healthy for the soul.

Suicide is the last resort of the lost.
It is where we go when we are desperate
   and have nothing to hold onto.
But it is not the answer you want or need.

You want the pain to end
   and the only way you know to kill the pain
   is to kill yourself.*

---

* This is an insight from my friend Beth.

The act of killing yourself will not end the pain;
    it will just recycle it.
You will come back to the same pain next lifetime
    to deal with it again.
        And the cycle will continue until you face it
            in its entirety.
There is no easy escape from this journey;
    truthfully, there is no escape at all from this journey—
    the only way is through.

So when you stand at the edge, know you are indeed in hell
    but you will not be here forever.
Know that you will have to go through this hell;
    there is no going around or going over
    or a bypass or a detour.
    Just through.
    And you can get through it.
So know you are not alone and know suicide is not the answer.

When you stand at the edge of this great abyss, face it.

Scars

Abuse often is scarless
leaving invisible gaping wounds that no one can see.

How can your childhood be so terrible
if you have escaped noticeable injury?

It is sometimes easier if there are scars
because then there is proof.

Scars on your heart, mind, and soul
offer no physical evidence.

Embrace and honor
the evidence that *is* present:
your knowing
your truth.

They give testimony to
the scars that do not show.

What scars do you carry that no one can see?
What truths do they speak?

Self-Work

All work is self-work.
This means every single, solitary thing that happens in your life
    is about you.
Don't be confused.
This does not mean you are the center of the Universe.

It means that every conversation, every encounter, every action
    has a lesson for you.
There are no accidents, coincidences, flukes, lucky breaks,
    flaws of fate.
    Your life is your classroom.

Something happens.
It brings your work to you as a gift,
    a gift of work you need to do on yourself.

Avoid the temptation to project the work
    onto those around you.
Elude the enticement to take everyone else's inventory for them
    so you can ignore your own.

Recovery makes self-work easier, not unnecessary.

If you are still breathing,
    you have self-work still to do.

What lessons are in front of you today?
Where are you embracing your self-work?
Where are you denying your self-work?

Releasing Captives

Forgiveness is healing a broken relationship.
It's the building of a bridge where, before, none was needed.

Forgiveness is removing any obstacles of resentment
    and bitterness.
It is lowering the walls of self-protection
    in order to enter the courtyard of vulnerability.
It's the willingness to embrace the other once again as friend.

But this is not the only description of forgiveness.

Forgiveness is releasing someone from the karma
    they incurred by their actions,
though it does not ever release them from the lessons
    they have to learn
    or from the lessons they decline to learn.

We choose our lessons each life.
While we can refuse to learn them
    we cannot un-choose them.

Forgiveness is releasing the attitude of perfection
    and embracing the reality of humanity
    and our often glacially slow progress.

Forgiveness does not mean you have to be in relationship
    with the other.
    You can release their karma and let them go
    with compassion.

If you hold others captive by your un-forgiveness,
    you are still maintaining a relationship with them.
Now you are the warden of their captivity.
    This may seem like power, but it is not.
    It is more a passive-aggressive abuse of power.
Authentic power names the brokenness of the relationship
    and seeks to mend the severed connection
    or
    seeks to end the relationship honestly.

Forgiveness is a choice.
    There are no guarantees or warranties.
    It cannot be demanded or faked.
You can choose to forgive the karmic debt
    but not be in relationship,
    or choose to forgive the karmic debt
    and rebuild the broken bond.

And for most of us, our main captive is our self.

We often struggle to forgive others
   because we cannot forgive ourselves.

Now is the time to release yourself.

   Whom are you holding captive?
   Where are you holding yourself captive?
   How can you release them?

Playing in Hell

Sucking silt is a particularly difficult stage to be in.
Gentleness is key.

Give your little kids the opportunity to play
while going through the hell of sucking silt.

Emotional
Tell your kids how much you love them.
Play with a kitten or puppy.
Tell your kids some truths about who they are:
 truths about their bravery, strength, determination, etc.

Spiritual
Write a poem to your kids about the value of life.
Watch a sunset in silence.
Visualize your kids wrapped in love: safe, protected, and secure.

Physical
Get some play dough and create.
Eat your favorite ice cream or other treat.
Paint or draw a favorite memory from childhood.
Play a childhood game you enjoyed.

Mental
Read your favorite children's books at bedtime.
Take a class you have always wanted to take.
Do some puzzles that your kids like.

4

CLIMBING *the* MOUNTAIN

Climbing *the* Mountain

At some point—
I don't know exactly when—
you will stop sucking silt and begin climbing the mountain.
The very worst, the most horrible aspect, is over:
   the shock, the overwhelming sense of one's world
   totally dismantled, is past.
Now, begin the climb over and out.

Climbing the mountain is just as grueling
   as earlier stages in its own way.

You will begin to climb the steep
   stony façade of the mountain,
   seeking handholds and footholds with each movement.
You will ascend with bleeding fingers, exhausted arms,
   toes cramped from holding your weight,
   legs screaming for oxygen,
   as you deal with the next level of memory fallout.

You are no longer sucking silt
   where memories are so very dreadful
   that you are numb with shock.

Now you are climbing the mountain of memories
   where you are not dumbstruck by depravity
   but in awe of the magnitude of your abuse.

This is your mountain.
Climbing is exhausting and lonely and slow.
   Sometimes you will climb fast and then get stuck,
     scared to ascend any further
     and terrified to rappel back down.

Then you will fall
   back to the bottom of the canyon.
Dazed by the drop,
   you acknowledge the memories are a difficult adversary.
   But, undaunted, you begin the climb again.

And again, the mountain is formidable.
You feel as if you are climbing entirely vertically
   and pain is ever present,
   but you know you are stronger.
And you know you can go further,
   past the spot where you fell last time.
Then you fall again back to the bottom.
You feel as if you were making progress only
   to have the memories overwhelm you
   and you fall back into hopelessness and despair.
This time you want to quit:
   the mountain of memories is too much.

It will be very tempting to lie on your back
    and give in and give up.

Don't.

You can conquer this mountain—
    climb it, crest it, stand on top.
You will climb and fall many, many times.
But you will conquer it if you persist.

If you try to quit, your children will not let you rest.
They are climbing with you, and they long for the summit.
It is impossible to stuff the memories back
    into unconsciousness,
    hide them, bury them without severe jeopardy.

The only way is to deal with them
    and that means you must climb the mountain.

Take as much time as you need, and do it as fast as you can.
Feel the depth of all the emotions, and don't dwell on them.
No matter what, keep climbing.

There may be multiple mountains.
    Memories will come in groups:
    you may think the mountain you are on is the only one,
    but then you will see another mountain in the distance,
        waiting for you.

Take them one at a time.
Each will have its challenges and lessons.
Know also that each one will have its own summit.
And when you crest that summit and stand tall on its peak,
    be proud of who you are,
        grateful for where you came from,
        and confident of where you are going.

Paradox *of* Life

The paradox that is life is sublimely evident
as you heal from abuse.

We feel horror at and affection for our abuser.

We hate them and love them at the same time.

We want them to live on another planet
but still want them in our lives.

We desire justice but want to protect them.

We feel guilty yet know we are innocent.

We are broken yet healing.

We believe wholeness is possible
but are not sure we will ever reach it.

We are lost and exhausted but refuse to quit.

When we embrace the paradox that is life,
we can let go of the dualism that things are either
right or wrong, good or bad.
They just are.

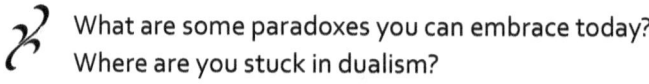 What are some paradoxes you can embrace today?
Where are you stuck in dualism?

Never-Ending Memories

It feels as if the memories will never end.
They keep coming and coming . . .
    when you are least suspecting and most vulnerable
    while you are walking down the hallway at work
    merging into rush-hour traffic
    reaching for a can of soup at the grocery store
    in the middle of a movie you've been dying to see
    as you mow the lawn
    just before you fall asleep.

Sometimes you are triggered by the most random things . . .
    the musky, masculine smell of cologne
    an old song from your childhood
    the look of your boss's smirk
    your lover's hand caressing secret places
        and the memories start to pour out . . .
            sometimes whole
            but more often in bits and pieces
            flashback snapshots that for years were deeply buried.

It feels as if the memories will never end
    as though you are trapped in your childhood
        powerlessly surrounded by abuse with no way out.

It feels as if the memories will never end—
    after all, it's been months and years of work now
        and still the memories come.

Now is the time to remember and savor your progress.
Even the smallest victories are still victories.
Let yourself recall and then sit with those successes.
They are real.
And their numbers will increase.

It feels as if the memories will never end.

But they will.

Shake *the* Dust *from* Your Feet

Many of us will find that significant relationships may change
   as we heal.
What do you want and what do you need
   from the various relationships you have?

Families can be biological.
Families can be chosen.
Just because you are related by blood
   doesn't mean you have to be in relationship.

You choose.

You do not owe someone a relationship.
   Just because you are a son or daughter,
      niece or nephew,
      grandchild, godchild, or cousin,
      there is no obligation on your heart.

If you need to end a relationship because of abuse,
   shake the energy from your being.
   Let go of the relationship with empathy and compassion.
      Do your best to avoid resentment or anger.

Trust your instincts of self-protection.

And remember, the relationship you have with yourself
   is supreme.
So choose yourself first.

Sometimes it just does not work.

Sometimes the energy just ends—
   no one's fault, it is just over.

Sometimes the relationship changes—
   and two grow in different directions
   one goes east, the other west
   one stops, but the other must continue.
Do not keep trying to revive something that is long dead.

We hang on out of fear:
   fear of being alone,
   fear of being unloved.

It takes much courage to even look to see
   if the relationship is worth the energy you are expending.
And still further courage to say good-bye.

When you get to that point
   do so with compassion
   for both yourself and the other person.

Do so with forgiveness for both your shortcomings.
Do so with understanding that you tried your best
    at this point in time.

Practice gratitude for the learning you gained
    from this experience.
Take that learning with you.
Then shake the dust from your feet and let it go.

Taking a Break

During the sucking silt stage there are no breaks.
You may want to quit but that is really not an option.
Sucking silt is life or death.

Climbing the mountain may allow for breaks.
Consider them conscientiously.

Listen to your body.
   It has done the heavy lifting of holding all the memories.
Listen to your mind.
   It often wants to take an escape route
      mistakenly believing that escape is possible.
   Don't be fooled by the attraction of taking a break
      if your real motive is evading.
Listen to your soul.
   It is your connection to the Divine
      and knows what you came here to do.
Listen to your little kids.
   Respect their sense of timing for work and play.

If you decide to take a break, enjoy it.
 Savor it.
 Allow yourself the rest that you deserve from memory work.

And when you're rested,
 return to the mountain.

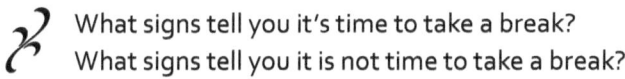
What signs tell you it's time to take a break?
What signs tell you it is not time to take a break?

Wants and Needs

Wants and needs are different
and
they both change as one heals.
Wants are desires, requests, luxury items
we wish to have in our lives.
Needs are necessities, requirements, essentials
for health and wholeness.
Both are unique to the individual.
What you want or need will be different from others.

Spiritual
Make a Wants and Needs list for your spiritual being.

Physical
Make a Wants and Needs list for your body and physical being.

Emotional
Make a Wants and Needs list for your emotional being.

Mental
Make a Wants and Needs list for your mental being.

5

RIDING *the* WAVES *of* HEALING

Riding *the* Waves *of* Healing

You are learning to feel,
   to deal with emotion.
Emotions are like water
   ebbing and flowing,
     white capping and calm,
     deep and shallow.

Learn to ride the waves of all the emotions
   as they present themselves.
Sometimes you will feel as if you're drowning,
   unable to catch any oxygen
   or even know which way the surface is.
Emotion can be powerful, overwhelming, daunting.
But it's just energy
   seeking an outlet after years of containment.

Remember you do not have to act on any emotion—
   just let it run through your body.
Be conscious of the lessons,
   learn what it has to teach you about yourself.

Some emotions may require action.
    Respond to each appropriately.
    Abusing yourself or another is just more violence to yourself
        that you will need to heal.
Odds are you did not learn many healthy methods
      of dealing with emotions in your family,
      so now's your chance.

Many of us permit our emotions to control us,
    allow rage to boil over, allow grief to paralyze us.
    But emotions do not control us
      if we are conscious of their presence.

You are in charge of and responsible for your emotions.
Always.

Healing Comes *in* Many Colors

It is RED . . .
    representing your passion
    as it begins to return and thaw and heat up.

It is ORANGE . . .
    like the rising sun
    that illuminates what your abuse may teach you.

It is YELLOW . . .
    a boldly penetrating, dazzling light
    that heals all wounds.

It is GREEN . . .
    when you find your heart and open it
    to the beauty and wonder that is you.

It is BLUE . . .
>   as the shackles of silence erode away
>   and your proud voice speaks your truth.

It is PURPLE . . .
>   exemplifying your deep penetrating vision
>   that sees your life unfolding as it is meant to.

What colors speak to you?
Draw or paint or color what healing means to you.

Healing *the* Body

You have a body.
You are a body.
A body: carbon, nitrogen, oxygen, hydrogen.
In other words—
   Earth
known as dirt, soil, dust.
And most often referred to as less-than, inferior, dirty, sinful.

But without a body, we could not feel.
It is the physical body that allows us the gift of emotion.
Spirits are pure energy—they do not feel.
Bodies hold and contain and transmit emotion.
So we have bodies *to feel*.

To feel is the ability to perceive
   passion and despair
   wonder and confusion

Without feeling, how would we know joy or serenity or awe?

So the point is not to contain the emotions—
    certainly not to deny them—
    but to experience emotions in their totality.

Emotions are not good or bad—
They just are.

And they exist in a pendulum-swinging state:
    The degree to which we are willing to experience pain
    is the degree to which we will experience joy.

So embrace emotions as the gift of the body.
Let your body feel them; let your mind acknowledge them.

Every single emotion and each memory are stored
    in our physical cells.

So as an adult, when you do memory work,
    your body will relive that trauma.
It is terrifying
    but necessary.

Your little kids need to be rescued;
    the memories need to be released;
    the body needs to be healed.

Perhaps you hate your body
    for being abused,
    for not protecting you,
    for being the target of another's violence.

Perhaps you don't even know you have a body:
    you just have a container you use to function in the world,
    as if it's a tool
    but not really you.

Your body has suffered along with your mind and your soul.
It needs tender attention to heal.

Own your body as the sacred Divinity of Earth
    equal to the soul
    grateful for its genius of experiencing the gift of emotion.

Twenty-Three Ways *to* Nurture *the* Body

Soak in a bath
Relish a massage
Walk along the beach
Smell your favorite flower

Hug a tree
Listen to chimes
Visit a rose garden
Listen to some silence
Go for a swing on a swing set

Listen to Mozart
Watch the sun rise or set

Eat a mint
Discover a beautiful rock
Meander barefoot on the grass

Visit a zoo
Play in leaves
Walk in the woods
Smell cinnamon or cloves
Savor some raspberries or strawberries

Hug a friend
Play with a puppy
Lie back on the earth and count the stars

Look in the mirror and say, "I love you."

 Make your own top twenty-three list.

Healing
the Heart

Healing the heart requires nerves of steel and unyielding focus
on feelings that have been buried deep within ourselves.
We want to believe that burying our feelings
will make them dead.
It will not.
The feelings will just wait for us
to be ready to uncover and deal with them.

Courage!
The only way is through.
Discover the emotions you may want to deny
and allow yourself
to *feel*.

Our temptation is to label the emotions as "bad"
and then immediately seek an escape from feeling them.
We pray for something to take their place;
we medicate ourselves in avoidance;
we attempt to rebury them even deeper.

Courage!
Name it. Face it. Feel it. Be healthy about it.

Let the emotion run through your body, through every cell.
Then decide if you want to keep it
or release it back to the Earth.

Once run through the body,
emotions find their place.

If they are still so strong that you want to push them away,
you have not dealt with them thoroughly.
There is still more work to be done.
Go dig, do more uncovering,
and discover what is still buried.

When emotions have run their course,
they find a place of rest.
Once owned and accepted,
they have found peace
at home
in you.

The following emotions are shared by survivors of abuse.
We all experience them to some degree.
On paper, the chart is linear.
In real life, emotions are neither linear nor straightforward.
And we consciously work
    to own, feel, understand, and express them
    in order to find wholeness.

Start Here		**Find This**
Fear	Face it	Serenity
Depression	Embrace it	Joy
Guilt	Forgive it	Laughter
Anger	Express it	Acceptance
Grief	Experience it	Openness
Hatred	Admit it	Compassion
Shame	Release it	Dignity

Facing Fear

For some of us who have endured severe abuse,
    fear is the dominant emotion.
Fear of everything:
    fear of being alone or being in a crowd;
    fear from being able to see the enemy
        but know they are near;
    fear of the dark—
        too much space for predators to hide in;
    fear of the light—
        too exposing, too revealing;
    fear of being seen—
        as weak,
        being just like them;
    fear of intimacy but dying from loneliness;
    fear of standing out but stuck in isolation;
    fear of the past that kills the present
        and eliminates the future.

Fear is so powerful, so controlling.
    This dread that you will do the "wrong" thing
    halts you from doing anything.

Facing fear is the only way to deal with fear.
   The. Only. Way.

Up to now, fear has been your dictator.
But it is time to face it and its many levels.

If you are afraid for your physical or emotional safety
   go someplace safe.
If you are in fear from your memories
   let them come and speak their truth.
Your little kids have lived in fear long enough.
You can be their knight, their superhero to protect them
   from whatever they fear.

Living in fear means hypervigilance, paranoia,
   and a continuous diet of adrenaline—
   hard on both the body and the soul.

But on the other side of fear is autonomous power
   and self-respect
   the main ingredients of self-knowledge.
And that is always synonymous with serenity.

Welcoming Serenity

Serenity means

saying "I'm sorry" without feeling
that you've been condemned to hell

accepting all the beauty and divinity of who you are

genuine peace

forgiving yourself for being who you are

letting go of resentments and revenge and jealousy

embracing the imperfections and flaws of your personality
as treasured parts of who you are,
not the totality of who you are

owning your abuse as reality not as an excuse

thanking the Universe for all your lessons, even the abuse

knowing who you are and knowing you are enough

How do you experience fear at this point of your healing?
How do you experience serenity at this point of your healing?
What helps you move from fear to serenity?

Embracing Depression

Depression
    a void with no doors,
    the black hole of emptiness
        where you're dead on the inside
        but still breathing on the outside.

It's the free fall into
    a biochemical breakdown
    a psychological paralysis
    a spiritual wasteland
    hell on earth.

Name it
own it
embrace it as the reality of your life at the present.

Try every possible healthy solution to manage your depression:
    meditation, exercise, community, hobbies.

When necessary, take medication to help.
Sometimes the feelings are too overpowering,
    and you need assistance managing them.
    That's okay.

Sometimes you want to medicate yourself to the point
    that you feel nothing at all.
    That's not okay.

For some, medication is their permanent resolution.
For others, medication is a temporary safety net
    over too turbulent waters.
Only you know which is your situation.

The point is to feel as much as you can
    without depression crippling you.
The healthy edge of healing is
    embracing the maximum ability to feel
    without compromising your progress.

The
Joy *of* Joy

It's the single drop of dew
   on a bright green blade of grass
   that blesses your leg
   as you stride down the well-worn path
   of the southern bank of the Mississippi River
   under a pink sky of fresh dawn.

It's the unqualified stillness
   of a full-moonlit moment
   that caresses your being with awe
   as you slip deeper into the blissful tranquility
   of the full experience of silence.

It is exploring the deepest regions of your soul
   and cherishing what you find.

It is the absolute knowing you are full
   of God.

Draw, color, or paint a picture of depression.
Draw, color, or paint a picture of joy.
Commit to creating at least one joyful moment every day.

Forgiving Guilt

"When you're wrong, promptly admit it."*

Knowing when you're wrong can be challenging.
- Were you wrong?   mistaken?
- malicious?   hurtful?
- mean?   passively aggressive?
- conniving?   oblivious of others?
- Was it intentional?   [more karma]
- unintentional?   [still wrong]

Sometimes we're not wrong; we just think we are.
    We apologize even though we are not wrong.
    We try to own things that aren't ours.
Analyze carefully.
    Own your wrongs; allow others to own theirs.

---

* Alcoholics Anonymous, Step 10.

The "promptly admit it" part needs a little explanation.
    "Promptly" as in now.
        Delaying may be attractive, but it is dangerous.
        We may talk ourselves out of doing what we need to do.
    Admit it without excuses or blame.

Being wrong is part of being human.
We make mistakes; we hurt others.
It's when we don't promptly admit it that we incur guilt.

Guilt's burden is heavy.
    And the burden grows in proportion to our denial of it.

The cure for this burden is:
    When you are wrong, promptly admit it.

Laughter

Laughter is the chocolate ice cream cone
   of emotional expression.
It is energy that starts to build deep within
   the tickling of intercellular tissues
   until it sneaks out in a smile
   then bubbles out into a giggle
   before finally erupting across the face in glee.

Laughter is not an emotion, but it should be.

What guilt do you need to release?
Where do you need to admit you were wrong?
What makes you laugh?

Expressing Anger

Anger is the rising fury and the sometimes silent fire:
    not an original sin—just a part of being human.
    not wrong—natural and healthy.
Use it
Feel it
Run it
WELL.

Healthy anger can drive you through the pain the fastest.
It is the best motivation to move toward healing.

You are entitled to your anger:
    you were hurt.
You are not responsible for your abuse;
    you are responsible for your anger.

Anger is the natural response,
    so be angry . . . WELL.

Like all emotion, anger needs an outlet.
Do not stuff anger
   It will just find an alternative route to its destination,
   which is out.

There is no "right" way to be angry.
Only one rule: anger must not hurt yourself, anything,
   or anyone.
You do not get to beat, humiliate, hurt, offend, wound,
   or abuse others
   because you are angry.
This only continues the cycle of abuse
   and gives you serious karma you don't need or want.

Our culture does not teach us how to be angry.
You can learn.
Practice.
Experiment.
Be angry
WELL.

Healthy Ways *to* Be Angry

Speak to the person you are angry with by saying,
    "I am angry with you because I . . . "

Punch a punching bag or pillow.
Break pencils.

Scream.
Go to the woods and break sticks.

Pound a basketball on the ground or into a wall.
Run as fast as you can for as long as you can.

Have a *pretend* conversation with the person you are angry at
    and be honest.
Hit a tennis ball into a wall.

Have a mock funeral for the person you are angry with.
Give a donation in your abuser's name to a rape or abuse center.

Swear into your pillow.
Use a tennis racket and pound your mattress.

Call your therapist.
Draw a picture of the person you are angry with
   and use it for dart practice.

Beat the sofa cushions.
Go for a walk.

Hammer on a two-by-four.
Write a letter to the person you are angry with
   but *do not* mail it.

Call a friend and say, "I am so angry because I . . . "
Lie face down on the ground
   and give your anger to the Earth . . .

The Gift *of* Acceptance

Acceptance is . . .

   The ability to love something as it is
      refraining from judgment at its present state of being

   Seeing things as they are
      not as you want them to be
      or as you hope they will be tomorrow

   Knowing the world is a beautifully harsh place
      a brokenly gifted place
      where everything in it is doing the best it can.

Acceptance is . . .

   patience, tolerance, empowerment
      welcoming the wounded
      kissing the warts
      embracing the broken
      forgiving the offending
      loving the struggling

What are you angry about at this moment of your healing?
What can you do to feel and release that anger?
Where are you openhearted and accepting?
Every day embrace and increase your acceptance of your little children.

Experiencing Grief Uncovered

Grief is covered up in our culture.
We often pretend it does not exist.
But it will wait like a long-lost friend—patient—
   to be uncovered and claimed.

If you ever have been angry, you have had grief.
Anger comes first, but it is always a secondary emotion.
   Always.
Anger always covers grief.

Behind anger is pain
and behind pain is lost hope.
And "lost hope" is another name for grief.

   We get angry when the dog has to go out
      and we hoped to just relax in front of the TV.
   We get angry if someone cuts us off in traffic
     because we hoped for a safe trip home
     instead of hitting our brakes.
   We get angry when our best friend lies to us
     since we hoped we had a better relationship than that.

We get angry when someone dies
    because we hoped they would remain with us
    just a little bit longer.

That's what grief is: lost hope—
   the pain that comes from losing that hope
   the emptiness now that hope is gone
   the overwhelming, inconsolable belief
     that hope will never return.

Grief runs rampant through our body, mind, and heart.
It feels devastating as it careens down its path,
   leaving nothing untouched, nothing unbroken,
   nothing whole.

No one likes grief;
   we think it makes us weak.
What it makes us is human.

Grief is the raw response to our own vulnerability.
If we allow it, grief is a deeply illuminating teacher.

It is proof we are intimately connected
   far beyond our individuality.

Grief provides us with a view of the depth and breadth
   of how much we can experience emotion.
It reminds us most about the importance of having a body:
   to feel.

When grief is covered, we deny our humanity,
   and ultimately we deny our identity.
And one can die in many ways from a broken heart
   of covered grief:
      seeking unconsciousness by medicating yourself with drugs
      imprisoning your heart in a concrete bunker
      wearing arrogance as a mask of pseudo-confidence

Grief longs to be uncovered.
Uncovering grief will eventually bring healing,
   but first you have to feel the pain.
Doing this is an act of maturity, an act of adulthood.

Your kids have been through hell and don't want any more pain,
But you must be the wiser one and enter the valley of grief.

There may be a temptation to stay in grief.
   For some, wallowing in it brings sympathy from others.

Again, this advice:
   "Take as much time as you need and do it as fast as you can."

There is an end to grief,
   a path out of the valley to the other side.
Let your heart do the walking
   down the path of experiencing grief uncovered.

Wide Openness

Like the sky
   broad and expansive

Like the horizon
   never ending and far-reaching

Like the ocean
   deep and extensive

Like lightning
   breaking open and blazing up

Like a mountaintop
   inspiring and panoramic

Like a heart
   pumping fiercely, in rhythm.

🎵 Whom or what are you grieving right now?
Find a song that speaks to your pain, and play it as many times as you need to until you feel finished for now.
As you let the grief heal, notice what is happening in your heart.

Admitting Hatred
and Knowing Compassion

Hatred is the absence of love,
a deficiency in caring about self and another.
It is a closed door
a dead end.
Hate poisons.
This is the arsenic to passion and vitality.
It sucks the life out of health and wholeness.
Hatred kills.

Compassion is the essence of Divinity,
an abundance of blessings for self and another.
It is an open door
a crossroad of opportunity and possibility.
Compassion revives.
It's the oxygen of passion and vitality.
Compassion breathes life into recovery and wholeness.
Compassion heals.

Where is hatred showing up for you?
Allow yourself to feel it deeply without guilt.
You can hold onto hatred for as long as you need it.
Make a list of those you hate, and bury or burn it.
You will know when you have felt enough hatred
and that hatred begins to ebb, making room for compassion.

Releasing Shame, Encountering Dignity

I feel responsible for the abuse.	I am responsible for my life.
I feel dirty.	I am pure.
I feel run-down and devalued.	I am built up and valued.
I feel worthless.	I am worthy.
I feel embarrassed about myself.	I am proud of myself.
I am unlovable.	I am loved beyond measure.
I feel humiliated by others.	I demand that others respect me.
My abuse identifies me.	I identify my abuse.
Shame.	Dignity.

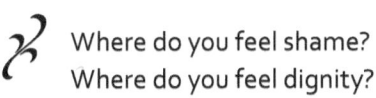
Where do you feel shame?
Where do you feel dignity?

The Serial Killer Called Resentment

This is not a test. This is an emergency!

Be on the lookout for the serial killer of recovery.
Goes by the name Resentment.

Identifiable aliases include jealousy, anger, bitterness, self-pity.

Claims to be a victim to anyone who will listen.
Is an expert at blaming others.

Likes to stalk, hiding in the shadows
   stockpiling bitterness as ammunition.

Has been seen often when self-pity needs to be fueled
   or when divisions can be furthered
   or when others can be injured.

Resentment is a threat to public safety and individual recovery.

If you encounter resentment, consider it armed and dangerous.
  Do not approach.
  Seek a place of safety, and avoid eye contact.
  Call your sponsor, your therapist, the fire department,
    911—
  call anyone who can help!

This is not a test. This is an emergency!

Healing *the* Mind

Healing the mind is the act of un-learning something old
   in order to learn something new.

The ultimate gift is that one's mind can always be expanded.
   The mind can be rewired through learning.
If you are still breathing
   you have something to learn.

What is it
   that is longing to be taken in?
What is it
   that longs to be learned
   and therefore acts as a center of transformation
   for your entire being?

Learn about your body—
   the most complex and intimate machinery
   that we play with daily.
Learn about your mind—
   its ability to un-learn and re-learn pathways, habits,
   attitudes, behaviors.

Learn about your soul—
    the eternal Divinity within you.

Learning transforms us
    from victims into whole human persons
    from lost souls into radiant beings.

You cannot heal without learning.
Be grateful for this gift.

It is a gift of the Universe that we have the power
    to re-create our lives.

The Reality *of* Brainwashing

Every act of abuse is an act of brainwashing.
Each violation shouts the repetitive misinformation
    that forms your mind in a way contrary to your true nature.

For children it is extremely difficult to not buy into
    the propaganda
    that is being shoveled so convincingly directly at them
    by the abuser.

Propaganda comes in many forms:
A slap means you are stupid.
A fondling means you are just a toy, someone else's sex toy.
A beating means you are not enough—
    you will never be enough to amount to anything,
    no more than a punching bag for someone else's rage.
A rape means you are an object, a tool for another's pleasure.

Each act has its own horror
    but what comes after every act of abuse is the brainwashing.
Your abuser doesn't even have to mouth the words
    for the deed will speak volumes.

Whatever the act, the message is that you are not worth
 anything.
 You are an object, not a person.

The more the abuse happens,
 the greater the effects of the brainwashing.
Soon you believe you are nothing but an object
 worthless
 useful only as someone else's emotional outlet.

None of this is true, but you will believe it
 because that is how you were taught.
Breaking the brainwashing will happen
 as you begin to reverse it.
Just as you were conditioned to learn negative,
 unhealthy patterns of thought
 you can program yourself to believe healthy affirmations.

This is not a feel-good platitude.
It is the stark reality of each and every creature on this planet.
 Everything has worth and dignity and value.
Healing the mind is the process of
 remembering that basic spiritual tenet.

A Plentitude *of* Affirmations

No matter who I am, I am lovable.
No matter what I did, I can be forgiven.

I have worth.
I am valuable.

Sex is beautiful
when I choose to participate with someone I love.
I can speak my truth.

I am safe.
I can make healthy choices for my life.

I am responsible for me.
I am my own hero.

All parts of me are beautiful.

I have gifts to share with the world that the world needs.
I can learn, un-learn, and re-learn what I need.

The Higher Power I believe in loves me.
I am good enough.

I choose to love.
I choose to dream.

I accept my past, embrace my present, and welcome my future.
I have power.

I belong here.
I am.

How are you programming yourself today?
What messages are you sending and receiving?
What messages do you want to send and receive?

When All Else Fails

When all else fails, learn something.

Something foreign and unknown—
learn the mysteries of its essence.

Something familiar that you cherish—
delve into the depths of its complexity.

Something you do not even think you'll like—
discover the secrets of its existence.

Learning shifts the energy in your body,
expands the mind,
refreshes the soul.

You do not know what you do not know
until you learn something.

And learning teaches you how little you know.

When all else fails, learn something
because learning empowers.

Healing
the Soul

You have a soul.
You are a soul.
The soul is your connection to the Divine
   the part of you that is Divine.

There are unlimited ways to define or identify the Divine:
   God, Higher Power, Energy,
   Pure Consciousness, Truth, the Universe,
   Wisdom.

You choose what or who the Divine is to you.

Mysticism is your inherent knowing
   and acceptance of the reality
   that you are connected to something beyond yourself.
It is your ability to be in relationship,
   to talk with and listen to the Divine.

All creation shares this ability because all creation is spiritual.

But being in this relationship is not easy.
It requires actions that are often contrary to our desires.

Being mystical means you have to shut up.
    Shut up so you can listen.
    Be still.
    Develop the art of embracing solitude
        of being with
        and listening to
        the spiritual world.

You have to be willing to sit on the floor
    in the corner of your basement
    weeping
    and totally alone
    in order to enter the Oneness
        that is just you and God.

Being mystical is the process of letting go of ego
    to surrender to Divinity—
    whatever you conceive the Divine to be.

It requires trust to let go of anything—
    especially ego.

You are part of the Divine but not the totality of the Divine.

In this relationship, you learn to yield to a Higher Power
    where respect is standard
    but equality is not.

Being mystical is your birthright.
It is who you are at your core.

The invitation is always open
   and it doesn't matter what you have believed
   or done in the past.

If you shut up, God will speak to you.

Spiritual work is hard because it is truly the work of adulthood.
It requires you to own your view of and relationship
   with the Divine.
There can be no hiding behind your parents' teachings
   or your church's dogmas.

It is you and God.
   And as Augustine, more than sixteen centuries ago, noted:
      We are restless until we find our home in the Divine.

The Dina Story

Several years ago I was driving from my house in Minneapolis to visit my sister in Alexandria, Minnesota. Having taken this trip many times, I always stop at the McDonald's in Monticello for a break. About five miles from the McDonald's exit, I heard this voice say, "Go to Wendy's."

I like Wendy's, but McDonald's was an easier stop, so I told the voice, "No, I don't want to go to Wendy's." Two miles later I heard the voice again, this time a bit more insistent: "Go to Wendy's." I tried to be firm, saying, "I don't think so." But the voice persisted. As I took the Monticello exit, I finally gave in.

I parked in front of Wendy's. As I opened the door to go inside, Dina, a good friend from high school whom I hadn't seen for almost a decade was coming out. What was astonishing is that Dina was living in Ireland and had just flown in for a family celebration. After recovering from our shock, we had a marvelous conversation before parting ways.

There are three morals learned from this story.
1) If you shut up, God will speak to you. You may hear a voice, see a vision, feel a conviction, and possess a sense of knowing.

However the Divine chooses to connect to you, the Divine will speak. Your job is to listen and discern.

2) There are times you will be asked to do what you do not want to do. But just as often, there will be moments of joy when the spiritual world blesses you with gifts beyond your imagination. The important part to remember is the "just as often" part.

3) You will not be fully alive or whole until you have a relationship with the Divine. You can run, but you cannot hide. The invitation is always present; the choice is always yours. And this partnership is absolutely essential for recovery.

The "No Visions, No Voices" Story

A woman I know told me this story about herself. When she was ten years old, she watched a video about Joan of Arc. Joan was a young French woman who talked to spirits and angels in her garden and was tried as a heretic by the Catholic Church. My friend said she decided at that moment that she never wanted any communication with the Divine like the one Joan had in her garden. So this woman declared, "No visions, no voices."

She journeyed through life and was attracted to a career in ministry. She wanted to be a chaplain, so she chose Harvard Divinity School to pursue a master's degree in divinity. After graduation, she began work in a large metropolitan hospital to complete her dream of becoming a chaplain.

Although she was very skilled in her profession, she knew something was missing. When she told me the story of her ten-year-old self declaring, "No visions, no voices," she could not or would not make the connection that the answer was her ten-year-old self's declaration.

She had closed a door, and she was the only one who could open it again. On the surface, this woman was successful; after all, she had attended Harvard! But she relied solely on her intellectual gifts and closed off her spiritual ones.

The spiritual world will not violate any decision we humans make. All doors remain open or shut as we wish.

Every being on this planet is a spiritual being. To ignore or disregard that fact is to ignore our birthright and to diminish wholeness. The fully alive person integrates body, mind, and soul. We may feel one part of us is "stronger" or better developed than other parts, but the doors to all must be open.

Consider carefully where you have said no to the Divine. No point in sinking into guilt—all humans have said no on occasion. Learn from the past; let it go; move forward.

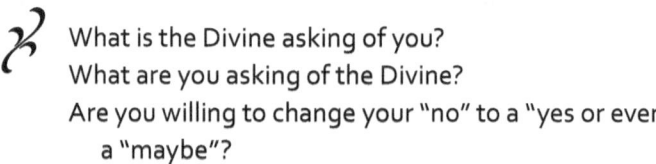
What is the Divine asking of you?
What are you asking of the Divine?
Are you willing to change your "no" to a "yes or even a "maybe"?

Praying

Prayer is the art of remembering who you are and who God is.
All effort that brings you closer to your Truth
    and therefore closer to the Divine
    is prayer.

Play with prayer.
It can be any gesture, action, position, word, thought,
    or state of being
    that connects you to yourself and the Divine.

When offering energy for others,
    be conscientious regarding how you pray.

It is easy to believe we know what another needs.
We may pray that someone recovers from surgery
    or gets well quickly.
But how do we know that is what they need?
Are we the Design Master of all creation?

We often play God with our prayers
    confusing what we want for another person
    with what they need.

To pray,
    ask that another receive and be open to receiving
    all that they need.

And that intention will always be
    more than enough.

Working Your Way to Wholeness

There is always something to work on;
as long as one is breathing, there is work to do.
One heals on the first level—
only to discover subsequent, deeper levels of the same issue
or a close relative of that issue.
That is a true test of growth:
healing on the deepest levels.

Emotional
Identify one or two emotions that you struggle to deal with
in a positive way.
Brainstorm ways to express these feelings in a healthier manner.
Play with these options, and explore which work best for you.

Mental
Identify one or two thought patterns that you struggle to deal with
in a healthy way.
Create a few healthy mantras you can play with and practice.
Read a children's book or poem to your little kids.
Write a book or poem for your little kids.

Spiritual
Identify one or two spiritual issues that you struggle to deal with
in a healthy way.
Discuss with friends or mentors and learn how others deal with
these issues.
Write a letter to the Divine, expressing who you are and what
you need.

Physical
What physical activities can you do when your emotions feel
overwhelming?
Play with these options, and explore which work best for you.

6

The ART of INTEGRATION

The Meaning *of* Integration

> Maybe it's because I look at everything as a lesson or because I don't want to walk around angry, or maybe it's because I finally understand: There are things we don't want to happen but have to accept, things we don't want to know but have to learn, and people we can't live without but have to let go.[*]

Integration is accepting that life is a paradox
    and accepting all the lessons that come with that truth.

It is embracing the memories
    when we long for a different childhood.

---

[*] Jeff Davis, Erica Messer, and Kimberly A. Harrison, "JJ," *Criminal Minds*, season 6, episode 2, directed by Charles S. Carroll, aired September 29, 2010.

Integration is loving a body
    that holds our memories we don't want
    and experiencing a heart
    that feels what we don't want to feel
    and surrendering to a soul
    that seeks beyond our own limits.

Integration ends the dualism of right and wrong
    stops compartmentalizing our existence
    into public and private facades
    and eliminates all our secrets
    letting everything be seen as reality.

We now stand at the summit of the mountain
    and can see the promised land
    of knowing and accepting who we are.

Integration is what we never had but have always longed for.

You charge forward, making great strides.

Then seem to go in reverse and lose ground.

You go backwards,
then plunge downward into places you thought
       you'd conquered.
  It feels like failure.
  You become depressed.

It is hard to be here.
Again.

Then a kind of neutrality happens.
  Waiting.
  An unknown divine secret timing.

Then you move rapidly. You charge forward.

And the cycle repeats.*

---

* Illustration concept by Beth Mahutchin.

Where Memories Go

Memories need a place of rest.
When we were kids, we just stuffed them
   anywhere they would go
   and tried like hell to forget those memories ever existed.

But the places we stuffed them into
   were not proper resting spots
   and the memories will not rest or give us peace
   until they also find a home.

It is easy enough to know if a memory is at rest.
When an individual memory has been thoroughly remembered,
   felt, and owned
   it will not speak to you or tug at you again.
It goes to the reservoir of lessons, where you can access it
   any time if you choose.

But the memory will not bother you again.
It is like finding the correct piece for its spot in the puzzle.
   It fits.
   Nothing else fits there
   nor does this piece fit somewhere else.
   It is home.

When a memory is not at rest
   it will tug, pull, churn inside of you
   until you acknowledge it
      until you claim it and its lessons as yours.

Memories long to go home
   to be welcomed in, cared for, laid to rest.

They are your pathway to wholeness, and they are you.

Friends *and* Enemies

Friends accept you; enemies try to change you.
Friends show up; enemies have other plans.

Friends challenge you to be whole when you want to quit;
   enemies pour you another drink.
Friends invite you to belong;
   enemies tear you apart from others.

Friends understand; enemies judge.
Friends hold you to the standard of recovery;
   enemies wonder why you need that in your life.
     (After all, aren't enemies enough?)

Friends stand by you; enemies stand apart.
Friends love you; enemies love themselves.

Perhaps "enemies" is too strong a word
   but what else do you call someone who stands against you?

When I Was Young

When I was young, I was arrogant and egotistical.
I was self-absorbed and incredibly self-righteous.

Because I was so lost.

I did not know who I was
   so I grasped onto external beliefs of others
      trying to make them mine
      trying to make them my identity.

Of course, other people's beliefs are not one's identity.

I had no clue that I was even wounded
   because my wounds were so deeply denied
   and my denial so deeply buried.

It had to be this way in order to survive—when I was young.

When I was young
   I was always on the outside looking in
   always needy
   desperately empty and pretending to be full.

Integration teaches me
    that young girl is me.
Integration teaches me *not*
    to ignore her
    or be embarrassed by her actions
    or pretend she is not my past.

When I was young, I was lost
    because I did not know who I was.
Integration teaches me that knowing who I am means
    embracing each young girl inside me
    and smiling at the wisdom and fortitude
    of every child within me.
    because each child suffered much and labored tirelessly
    to get me to today.

Different Worlds

As you integrate your past and present
   as you walk in your truth
   it may seem like there are different worlds
   operating at the same time.

There are some worlds where truth is not spoken.
   These worlds may consist of single individuals
      (a family member, a friend, a coworker or boss)
   as well as groups of individuals within systems
      (government, businesses, churches, schools).

Worlds of untruth are places where truth is not the priority—
   especially your truth.
You may feel minimalized, ignored,
   and invisible as you walk in your truth.

Those walking in this world of untruth cannot bear
   the presence of truth
   so they consciously or unconsciously hide
   behind defensive walls.

These walls have been built, maintained,
   fortified, and refortified
   by people who have let fear dictate their lives.

Truth will not violate their walls—
   that would violate the principles of truth.
No, truth is patient at the edges
   awaiting their willingness to grow.
It is always one's choice to walk in truth or walk in untruth.

So if you work with or live with or are related to
   those walking in untruth
   begin by acknowledging you are entering the world of denial.

At first you may just notice the feelings of anxiety—
   something is off, but you don't know what.
You may want to turn and run away—
   this world is not conducive to wholeness.
Sometimes you can leave. But sometimes you must stay.

When you have to stay in the worlds of untruth, be gentle.
Fear is the major player in this arena.
Be gentle with yourself and all who choose this world.

Then there are some worlds
   where we share an experience with another
      and we emerge with different truths.

Perhaps your family members remember the abuse
    differently than you do.
Possibly they have a different way of coping with it.
Probably they have a different lesson to learn than you do.

Walking in your truth means accepting
    that others do not have to follow your path.

Your truth does not depend on another's recognition of it.

This is a difficult part of healing:
    to stand secure in your truth
    and allow others to stand in theirs
    even if those truths are incongruent.

Integration means to walk and speak the truth
    in all areas of your life
    while doing the self-work that is in front of you.
    It also means accepting the reality that others
    may reject your truth.

Of course, this is an arduous process of effort
    and commitment.
So again, be gentle.

And if you should find yourself caught up
    in some world of untruth
    acknowledge your humanness and return to your truth.
Because you have walked in your truth
    you can always find truth again.

To walk in truth is painstakingly difficult
    yet rewarding beyond expectation.
Although the world of truth does not promise ease or
                convenience
    it guarantees wholeness.

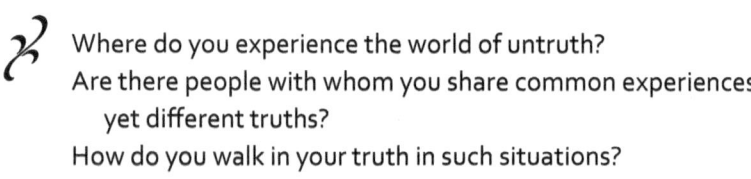 Where do you experience the world of untruth?
Are there people with whom you share common experiences
    yet different truths?
How do you walk in your truth in such situations?

Speaking Wholeness

Delete This	Build This into Your Vocabulary
I quit . . .	I will . . .
I can't . . .	I can . . . I can't do that, but I can do this . . .
I hate . . .	I do not like . . .
I worry . . .	I let go . . .
I should . . .	I am doing the best I can . . .

Living Consciously

Strive to be conscious
of your totality
in every aspect of your experience.

Seek to be present to your life in every moment.

Mental   Spiritual   Physical   Emotional
Work on taming your mind by sitting in silence.
Visit a religious community you are interested in exploring.
When you exercise, integrate your mind and soul into the experience.
Cultivate a healthy balance in your life.

7

The

PROMISED LAND

The Promised Land

The Promised Land is not a place of perfection
but the long-sought enjoyment and satisfaction
   of spiritual progress.

It is not a state of geography, but a state of being.

The Promised Land is not the absence of pain
   but the ability to take pain in
   acknowledge it, own it, befriend it, mourn it, heal it,
   transform it.

It is not a life free of suffering
   but a wholeness forged from suffering.

It is not a place where memories no longer exist
   but an attitude that knows memories are no longer a burden.

The Promised Land is not a location to escape to
   but a haven where memories' scars bear witness
      to formidable strength, incredible courage,
      and fierce determination.

It is where you know that
    even if someone hurts you in the future
    you will not be crushed;
    even if someone abuses you in the future
    they will not win;
    you will not be lost.

The Promised Land is where you know
    you are sacred and holy and divine and human and whole.

It is where you know who you are.

The Promised Land is not a land but a birthright.
The Promised Land is home.

The Promised Land's Reflection *of* Truth

You cannot be someone else.

You cannot take someone to a place where you have never been.

You cannot teach someone something you do not know.

You cannot heal if the wound is not exposed
and thoroughly scrubbed cleaned.

You cannot experience paradise until you've traversed hell.

You cannot be whole until you claim all the pieces of you.

Look at your journey. Consider how far you have come. What are your milestones of truth?

Rural Minnesota

					I am a drop of water
					in a miniscule creek
					in rural Minnesota
			that is flowing into an unnamed tributary
					of the Chippewa River
					south of DeGraff
				that joins the Minnesota River
					near Granite Falls
			that merges into the Mississippi River
					at Pike Island
		that flows downstream to the Gulf of Mexico
				near New Orleans, Louisiana
					that meets the Divinity
				known as the Atlantic Ocean
			that joins the Pacific, Arctic, and Indian.

I am a single soul
taking a body
in rural Minnesota
to learn how to be human:
in the face of abuse
on the farm
that led to addiction
that got me cutting my wrists
in a drunken despair
where I chose to face my life
rather than die
and return to learn it again
that led me through hell
until I found myself—
the Divinity within my Humanity.

My Creed

I believe in me.
I believe I am flawed and full, struggling and whole.
I believe in a Divinity that is Truth and invites me to be Truth.
I believe in the fullness of humanity
despite our cruelty and brutality.
I believe that all creation is fully Divine and fully Earth.

I am valuable, and I have worth.
I am free.
I speak my truth.
I walk my path.
I bear witness for myself.

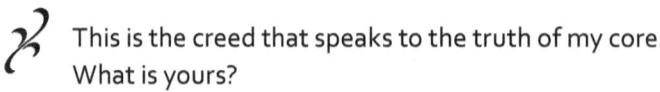

This is the creed that speaks to the truth of my core.
What is yours?

Found

There will always be a longing
   a hunger
   a pain
   a hurt
     from what was not.

But it is no longer what you lead with.
It is just part of you now—
   not the overwhelming and consuming drive it used to be.

It has made you stronger.
It has made you deeper.
It has been your path to wholeness.

Your wounding is no longer an obstacle
   but a blessing
   and the place where you can embrace
   your little kids with fierce devotion.

You have been through hell
    and emerged on the other side
    liberated.
You have found yourself.

Welcome Home.

Healing the World

Spiritual   Emotional   Mental   Physical

How can I
give back
and
share my recovery
to heal the world?

www.ingramcontent.com/pod-product-compliance
Lightning Source LLC
Chambersburg PA
CBHW032038290426
44110CB00012B/864